I0528238

BONE
— & —
STARS

*A Constellation of Poems of Healing
and Recovery from Narcissistic Abuse*

ERIN AURELIA

The cover art for this book is by Shellie Johns
You can connect with Shellie at
https://www.facebook.com/shelliejohnsart

———

© **2024 ALL RIGHTS RESERVED.**

Published by She Rises Studios Publishing **www.SheRisesStudios.com.**

No part of this book may be reproduced or transmitted in any form whatsoever, electronic, or mechanical, including photocopying, recording, or by any informational storage or retrieval system without the expressed written, dated and signed permission from the publisher and author.

LIMITS OF LIABILITY/DISCLAIMER OF WARRANTY:

The author and publisher of this book have used their best efforts in preparing this material. While every attempt has been made to verify the information provided in this book, neither the author nor the publisher assumes any responsibility for any errors, omissions, or inaccuracies.

The author and publisher make no representation or warranties with respect to the accuracy, applicability, or completeness of the contents of this book. They disclaim any warranties (expressed or implied), merchantability, or for any purpose. The author and publisher shall in no event be held liable for any loss or other damages, including but not limited to special, incidental, consequential, or other damages.

ISBN: 978-1-964619-65-1

PRAISE FOR BONE & STARS

"Like the phoenix that rises from the ashes, Erin Aurelia's debut poetry collection, *Bones & Stars*, is an unrelenting testament to the liberating power of poetry, music and community, and is a severe reminder that abuse can and does happen to the most giving of us. Rage with Erin as she shatters a complex past filled with grief, resentment, and denial, and transmutes her pain into a lyrical frenzy of empowered passion. Then, witness her rebirth as she removes the spoon of a sacrificial feeding and changes it out for a pen on fire, recovering her soul and her sanctuary, one fistful of poems at a time."

—Morgan Paige, poet, visual artist, entrepreneur, author of *Lick the Psychic: Poems by Morgan Paige*, from Lightship Press, and co-host of the Ghost Town Poetry Open Mic in Vancouver, Washington. Find Morgan online at www.lickthepsychic.com.

"Erin Aurelia's collection *Bone & Stars* showcases the rollercoaster of emotions and states of being when in and after an abusive relationship, the defeatedness and the pulling of one's self back up out of the darkness, the learning and relearning what is one's truth, the pain of being put in a low place and how much it hurts to dig out of it as well, like in the lines *spoke to me words / soft as gold* in the poem "Diamonds," and *there is a ghost in / this house / painting corners with / cobwebs* and *she breathed stars into her cells* in "Haunted.""

Erin creates scene after scene that puts the reader alongside this journey as every metaphor that is used for the abuser evokes the sense of being surrounded, helpless, and overtaken until she writes our way out with the voice of these poems, as in the poem "Eyes" that shows us, *those eyes feasted on my death / feasted / on my brokenness* and how the poem "Sweet Rain" begins with, *You didn't come.*

By the end of this collection, Erin has hauled her voice, along with us, down through the underworld and back up with a newfound strength and a rebuilt confidence. This collection is best consumed all at once to receive this energy: *I am not the carnage / rotting in the heat, / I am the lion.*

—Rebecca Smolen, poet, writing coach, private editor, Gateless Method Facilitator, and author of her chapbook, *Womanhood and Other Scars*, from The Poetry Box. Her writing is most recently found in the *Unchaste Anthology, Vol. 2 & 3*, *Mutha Magazine*, *VoiceCatcher*, and forthcoming in *Poeming Pigeon-Cosmos*, and *Shout*, the anti-fascist anthology from Not A Pipe Publishing. Find her online at www.rebeccawritespdx.com.

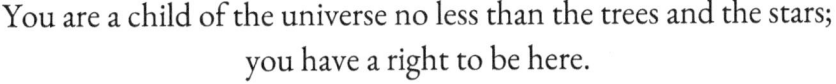

You are a child of the universe no less than the trees and the stars;
you have a right to be here.
—Sylvia Plath, *The Unabridged Journals Of Sylvia Plath*

To Sylvia Plath,
for awakening my burgeoning voice
and showing me how to make beauty out of sorrow.
Your words kept me alive in the dark.

To Pearl Jam,
for bringing my voice back after it fled
and showing me there is beauty in rage and pain.
Your music revived and resurrected me.

To my Open Mic Family,
for supporting and encouraging my returning voice
and for showing me the beauty of artistic belonging &
collaboration.
Your ongoing support means the world to me.

I wouldn't be here without you all.
Much love.

PRELUDE

TAPROOT

one taproot left

the others
starved
burned
withered
beneath
the gnarled
trunk

one left

still touching
living land
still breathing
deep oxygen
still
sonically
finding
secret
water

CONTENTS

PROLOGUE

THE MYSTIC

Sheets of mist
wrap around bare branches,
their reflection dim
in the colorless pond.

Snow the shade of
old memories falls
listlessly like a
used wish,   abandoning
the sullen gray sky.

Drifting wind
wanders restlessly
like a lost thought
with no existing words
to claim it.

A faint tune of
melancholy notes
floats through the fog—
the sun is nowhere to be found.

–Erin, age 15

INTRODUCTION

Words create and define the world we live in.

I wish I'd known the words *narcissistic abuse* decades ago.

I also wish I'd known the words *Narcissistic Personality Disorder (NPD)* and *covert narcissist*. And I wish I'd known that domestic violence doesn't only mean hitting. I didn't know these things when I was young and fell in love with someone who I thought loved me too, because of all the wonderful things he said to me and how much he seemed to want to spend time with me.

I didn't know the words *love bombing* back then, either. Or *intermittent reinforcement*. Or *emotional abuse*. Or *gaslighting*.

I didn't know that battered women were not always physically battered, but could also be emotionally, verbally, or psychologically battered.

Without knowledge, witnesses, or scars, for a long time, I had no idea what was being done to me.

Until I learned new words.

For two decades, I'd lived in a world where I was married to a good man who loved me but didn't seem to understand the way he sometimes emotionally hurt me and our sons, and if I could just explain it to him the right way, so he'd finally see, he'd stop.

And then one day I learned new words and found myself in a new world, in which I was living in domestic violence with a covert narcissist who was willingly, intentionally abusing me emotionally, and manipulating me by sometimes displaying seemingly kind and loving behavior so I'd stay and provide him with what he wanted—someone to bully so he'd feel superior, and who would adore him while he did so.

When I learned these new words that showed me the world I was actually living in, I left it.

I threw myself into trying to understand what I'd endured. I read everything I could about NPD and narcissistic abuse. I took domestic violence classes and attended domestic violence support groups at the YWCA. I attended Codependents Anonymous (CoDA) meetings. Gradually, the pieces of the puzzle of my past slid together and created a picture of what I had been living with and how to not repeat the experience.

I have not repeated the experience.

But then I was going through divorce with this abusive covert narcissist, which was a whole other experience to navigate. If being married to him was hard, divorcing him was harder, as he no longer wore any mask with me. His bullying became open and naked, and even though I'd left him, my voice still quavered in response.

Healing takes time. As does recovering one's voice.

In my youth, I'd written poetry prolifically. I began at an early age, writing light pieces for fun. When I reached high school and the special darkness that is being a 15-year-old girl who fears the powerful emotions and strange thoughts she experiences at that age, I discovered the poetry of Sylvia Plath and wrote pages and pages of poetry as I navigated that inner darkness I found myself in. Writing poetry was my expression and my salvation.

I wrote poetry as naturally as breathing.

I didn't realize then that poetry is my native language.

Less than a decade later, that voice faded to mute.

I'd learned, as our society conditions girls, to capitulate myself to boys and men to gain love. But I also encountered a covert narcissist who used his charm to both entice and confuse me, and this subtle unsettling left me unsure of my voice. It wavered, quavered, then eventually went silent.

I didn't write poetry for twenty years.

I didn't realize then that this meant more than simply not making art. I didn't realize then that not making art was the result of having capitulated my voice and power. I didn't realize then that no longer writing poetry had rendered me dead inside.

I didn't realize then that I had become the walking dead, until I came back to life in an unexpected way.

Music saved me.

Months after having left my marriage home, I reconnected with the music of a band I'd followed in my youth after I saw a photo of their frontman on social media. The band is Pearl Jam.

I recalled listening to their music when I'd moved out of my childhood home as a young adult. I revisited their early songs that reminded me of this independence, which I was suddenly encountering again at midlife, and needing to channel to keep myself going.

Months afterward, they posted live videos from their Home Shows concerts in Seattle. When I watched and listened to their performances, something profound occurred within me, as can happen when encountering art, because art is a holy mystery:

I wrote a poem.

It came in a sudden rush of heat and a tumult of words that spilled from my pen, and then, like an exhale, it was done.

I'd not written like that in two decades.

I had not heard these particular arrangements of words before, but I recognized the voice. It sounded like that of a long-lost sister returning home. This very first poem that revived my voice is the second in this collection, called "Silent Scream."

The next night, I watched more posted videos, and to my delight, I wrote another poem.

The following night, I wrote another one.

In the magical way that art can, this music suddenly opened wide my long-stopped spigot, and for the next several years, I again wrote prolifically.

So many feelings I had unknowingly numbed myself to in order to survive my abuse suddenly awakened, and I began to feel *all* of them. They needed some way to come out, some kind of release, somewhere to go.

They needed words so I could properly see and know them. They needed poetic words, as only the language of poetry is strong enough to convey and contain their energy.

I excavated the wreckage of my inner self that had endured abuse for so long. I needed words to explore and grasp what this abuse had done to me, as I lacked any physical marks to tell me the story.

Abuse and *violence* were the words I began with. These are graphic things, and I required graphic words to paint a full picture of and fully understand what had been done to me.

The deeper I went, the more words I heard and wrote. Writing these poems felt like pulling off mounds of debris from my barely-breathing body that had become trapped beneath the rubble of a collapsed mine shaft.

I resuscitated and resurrected myself as I wrote them.

And music continued to save me.

After months of immersing myself in the full catalog of Pearl Jam's music and frontman Eddie Vedder's solo music to fuel my poetic writing, I suddenly heard a clear inner voice tell me, *You need LIVE music.*

I wasn't sure why, but it sounded fun. I was driving to the grocery store when I heard it. As I arrived and parked and stepped out of my car, my ear caught the strains of guitar and singing. It grew louder as I walked toward the store. When I reached it, there standing out front was a young man, busking. *Live music!*

I stopped and chatted with him, and dropped a fiver into his open guitar case. I told him I like Pearl Jam and he showed me his Kurt Cobain tattoo, then played me a Glen Hansard song that I sang along to. I asked him if he knew where to find live music in town. He was still too young himself for many local music venues, so he told me he attended an open mic he enjoyed at a downtown coffee shop. He also said there was a website I could find online that listed all the open mics happening around town.

I was thrilled to get this lead and once back home, immediately began investigating. I discovered local open mics for writers and poets, as well as for musicians, and began exploring them all.

I visited the first two music open mics on the list and didn't really resonate with them, but at the third, I found one I enjoyed that featured a great array of artists. I listened to them play and wrote poetry as I did.

Then one night the host invited me to share my poetry on the mic. I was excited to be invited to perform in a venue mostly featuring musicians. I read three poems. After I read, he and other musicians there cheered my work and encouraged me to come back and read again. To my surprise and delight, this host even invited me to create a song with him from one of my poems; he told me my poetry sounds musical. It is featured in this collection, called "Light Speed, a song."

Soon after, he began accompanying me on his guitar as I read my poems onstage. In this, I discovered a new joy—not just listening to live music, but performing my poetry *to the accompaniment of live music,* which created a live soundtrack for my powerful emotions and words. I began performing with various musicians at different open mics, and together we created new art and new listening experiences in the process.

This artistic collaboration is the magic that was calling me to find live music, to not only inspire my writing, but to enliven my performances, which deeply supported my journey of healing and recovery.

I also discovered a longstanding poetry open mic that warmly welcomed me into their community, where I connected with and thrived among other passionate poets. I marveled at how perfectly these communities were available to catch and support me when I ran from the only life I had known here for so long, how if I hadn't followed the boy here who ended up nearly destroying me, I wouldn't have met these amazing artists who were willing to hear and support me as I revived and resurrected myself through writing poetry.

I learned that artists need the company and influence of other artists to thrive.

In all of these venues, speaking aloud the words I had written enacted an entirely new level of healing within me. Giving them sound, sounding the emotions they describe and with which they were written, sent powerful waves of energy through me. Being accompanied by the sounds of music enhanced this experience.

Poetry was my process but is also my path. One poem at a time, I sang my way home to myself.

Hearing my voice aloud reminded me I wasn't invisible, as I'd so often felt, and those who listened to me perform reminded me of the same when some shared with me how deeply my words had moved them and how they related, having endured similar situations themselves.

I found power in all of these modes of expression, through writing and performing words, being heard, and connecting with listeners, and each mode offered its own unique gifts.

I also began realizing that these words weren't only for me, that they are a wider medicine that isn't only mine.

This book and these poems are for readers who have experienced narcissistic abuse themselves and are on their own journey of healing and recovery, to offer support on their way and let them know that they are not alone. You will survive and thrive.

It is also for those who may be experiencing narcissistic abuse but are unfamiliar with the term and unaware that they are experiencing it, as I once was, to help them recognize their experience and know that it isn't their fault. You can leave and recover yourself.

We are all warriors fighting our way back to ourselves against forces that conspire to smother us.

We are all phoenixes resurrecting ourselves from the fires they thought would destroy us.

And despite their best efforts to hold us down,

We

Are

Rising.

RIVERNESS

One by one, knowing birds lift
    themselves from a riverbank
        laced with snow

Hours and days and eons forged
    from the mud beside the water
        are carried away in their beaks
        until

all that remains is
    current and bone
    eddies and marrow
    reflections and terror
        like a mirror reposing
        like a corpse
        adrift

When you plunge your
    hands into its flow and
        stare down into its depths,

do you know who you are if
    your visage retracts, if your
        image refracts into the

myriad colors welling up from
    the land that breathed you
        whole?

Will you know who you are when
  the river steals your voice and
    sighs in your place. while
      wearing the face you
        present to the world
        and have come to believe you
         own?

Are you remembering your name when
  the thoughts in your veins have been
    dispassionately bled and the silt of
      the river fills those caverns instead?

Your eyes cannot help you
  here, nor can your ears

only your tears that speak
  river-tongue can assuage
    your untenable fears as

riverness
drowns
your
illusions
in
her
coldly
loving
arms

SILENT SCREAM

thunder under cover
rage caught in lungs
lightning shot through veins

tasting bitter sulfurous sounds
rumbling, rambling under my breath
chewing on charcoal, smoking
to the skies

so much lost
so much to gain
right here, there is a silent storm
only drums and growls can quell

beating it out of me
beating it into me
beat by beat
measure by measure

tearing
rendering
furying
smiling
managing
faking
pretending
numbing
muffling
stuffing

stumbling

plunging into fecund soil like heaven's bolt—
charging barren land
stirring electrons into froth

light eaten by darkness—
what will grow here?

will it finally scream?

SHELTERED IN PLACE

inside
this dark
cocoon
sheltered
in place
i conjure
with stars
i sing up
wings
to adorn
my furry
form
i create
blindly
guided by
Arcane
knowing
arising
from the
reliquary
of my
Heart
and these
wings,
they are
just the
start
of what
this
Art
will forge

DIAMONDS

Yes, you put a diamond on
     my finger,
then spoke to me words
     soft as gold,
     cold as stone

Your lying love cut me deep
     like a backhand
     to the mouth
  laced with glass –

That diamond flayed my flesh
     one tiny cut at a time
     til it hung in ribbons
       about me
     and the tang of blood clung to me
       as I walked

My blood.

My blood falling out of me
in a million tiny rivers,
       slaking your thirst
       for iron –
     iron like the nails you spewed
     when you spoke to me last,
       looking for bone
           to land

So I walked out into the black night,
        leaving bloody footprints
                on your porch
        and that diamond in your dirt.

And as I stepped into the dark,
I was embraced by Stars that
        fell to meet me,
                to cloak me in diamond light
Shimmering like the northern aurora,
        blazing at my feet,
        and cutting me
                an iridescent path
                        to freedom

DENIED/DENIAL

nobody told me this was
  happening—
no sign, no signal,
  no warning flag

nobody told me i was being
  murdered—
suffocated, drowned, shot
  repeatedly

that I was bleeding out
  innards in pools about my
  feet, slippery beneath me

i walked past everyone
  smiling stupidly
with a snapped neck and
  severed digits

heard no voice call out
  tell me that i was leaving
internal organs in my wake

all the blithe faces
  grinning at me said, all is
   well
  you are well
   you're fine

this is fine.

even while my eyeballs hung
from their sockets
       and
rivers of pus ran from my
       ears

not until i heard thunder
       rumble in the distance, and
move in on the horizon
       did i notice,
while sitting in a ditch,
that i could no longer move,
as i was now a jumbled pile
       of dismembered limbs with
       skin slowly falling away

hey! i called to passersby.

oh hello, they said.

and kept walking.

HAUNTED

There's a ghost in
    this house
painting corners with
    cobwebs
because she's forgotten
    her name

Killed so softly—
    the blades brushed
oh, so gently over
    her thin skin—
she barely knew the
    difference between
life and death

the air was scarce
    either way, and
        just as rank

With each fresh cut,
    delivered with a smile,
        a memory drained
            away

swallowed up by
    he who wielded the knife—

a butcher of souls.

No one suspected the
      slow murder,
least of all herself—
      and so, like a
         leech

he grew fat on her
      blood
and she slowly faded
      from sight

Others swore they saw
      her,
heard her voice—
      just dry leaves
twisting and rasping in the
      wind
just reflections in
      the glass
teasing their eyes

Stumbling in the dark, she
      cried out, and was
shocked to hear herself,
      angry and indignant,
registering pain

Reaching reflexively to
      the wound, her hand
found the leech,
      firmly attached, and

she ripped it free

with glee she swallowed
          it whole—
felt warm blood
          flush her skin

saw her eyes stare back
          from the glass
                    bright, alight

tasted the tang of iron
          on her plumped tongue

and felt a heartbeat thrum
          again in her marrow

She breathed stars into her cells

and lit up her nights
          with living flame
                    til she burned so hot

that house burned down around her
          and she fired
                    her own path
                              to freedom

EYES

If looks could kill, they say—
        those eyes were serial killers,
            slaying me daily

cutting glances pierced me
        with judgment

sardonic stares stabbed me
        with contempt

following, assessing,
        calculating, criticizing,
crushing with the weight
        of everywhere—

even that charming visage,
        sparkling like glitter, was
raining jagged glass down on me,

as that smile was laced
        with cyanide
        masquerading as a
strawberry dipped in sugar

that beamed below reptilian orbs
        coldly injecting me
        with poison that
ate me alive from the inside out.

Those eyes feasted on my death
      feasted
on my brokenness
      sucked marrow from
      my bones
like a parasite
      until
my very cells
      ran dry
         and lay
            warped.

Darkness was resurrection, though.

When those eyes slept like
      vampires in coffins
I stood out beneath
      the night sky
covered in the stellar blanket
      of a thousand stars
smiling warmth into my soul

shining me whole

through a million lofty eyes

of light

REMEMBER

remember that pretty, gossamer words
      can be pretty, gossamer lies
      can be deftly disguised by
      razor blade lips that will cut
            when they touch you

remember that promises can be made
      even when unspoken, and can
      just as glibly be untied like
          snaking shoelaces

remember that even when enduring the
      pummeling of dark words and
      black glances that you are a fierce
      light so bright that you can banish
      their illusion of heavy, empty midnight

remember that when silenced, you still
      have a voice, and that it can
      reverberate and resonate
      like shattering glass
      like a screeching cat
      like an aluminum bat
          cracking against a ball
      like a breaking plate hurled
          against a wall

remember that the door that sucked you
      in like a vortex can be exited at

will
even though it might feel
like betrayal
or that your will may
grow stale
or that the very act would
impale your own heart

remember that every moment is
a sunrise, a fresh start
when you can begin anew
begin again
gather yourself and run toward
that horizon
remember to swallow sunbeams daily
to restore your sight
to lift you from quicksand and
to fortify your flight

INVISIBLE

incognito
where'er i walk
      banging on walls
      writing on rocks
      shaking trees
      throwing the wind with two fists

did you see it?
      or feel it?

tremors unfelt
growls unheard
voice emptied into darkness
      without echo
      eaten up by vastness
         by closeness

pressed, held down
      lightning smothered
      flames choked

is this oblivion a
      sentence or a lie?

uncertainty pricks and
      exacerbates
as i sink deeper,
      deeper down
into this violet-lit cavern,
watching faces float by

unreaching, ungrasping

am i here?

signals are weak
ambiguously sent, as
        they may not be received

am i here?
am i there?
am i anywhere?

RIGGED

In the stillness,
        I listen

Beats falling,
        dropping, pulsating
        gyrating
        masquerading
        confiscating
        obfuscating

And so I tear them
        aside
open wide the maws
        of fate
do not hesitate to
        reconstruct
        deconstruct
        resurrect
the contents of the
        everlasting
all the while understanding
        that we all stand
                on trap doors

the floor is rigged

watch
your
step

SWEET RAIN

You didn't come.

I sat in the rain
    under blackened skies

bones soggy with fear
    so full of it the marrow
    had leached out long ago

Promises were made
    I had been given to understand

but they were lies
    the skies told when
    the sun shone

Bedazzling light deceives
    wears sharp points—
    sunrays like teeth
    punctured my skin

(Sweet rain, let me in)

In your absence
    the rains came
    and so I welcomed them

and their clarity
that welcomed me

with their ferocity

and drove me down a marrowful river
     as the storm called my name

My bones know now you'll never come,
     but my ears are no longer
          pitched to your voice

I've decided to become the lightning, and
     take the thunder for my lover instead

THERE WAS SUPPOSED TO BE

There was supposed to be Heart,
       with full, resonant signals like
       arms cradling and caressing mine

There was supposed to be Soul,
       calling out to mine, recognizing,
       connecting, communing through time

There was supposed to be Fire,
       lighting you up, shining through you,
       and feeding mine, with joy

There was supposed to be Thunder,
       speaking Truth, clear and strong
       through the fog of uncertainty

There was supposed to be a Wind
       communing with trees and clouds
       carrying my kite with willing care

There was supposed to be the wide
       deep Sea—
       all-encompassing, breathing around us,
       holding us in that sonic silence of each
           cresting moment

It was supposed to be Fierce,
       not fallow,
       Complete,

not hollow
Fathom-ful,
not shallow
More Light—
less shadow
More Voice,
less echo.

There was supposed to be Trust
    not trickery

Less danger, more Safety

Now

there will be Rain
    beating, driving, drumming,
    washing all this away

There will be Rain
    fresh and clear
    scenting the air with renewal
soaking my ground of being
    with clarity

falling on every moment I breathe in
    Realization
Singing its calling song
    calling me home
    calling me home
    calling me home

to the sunlight through stained glass
      of color and peace
and the breeze through leaves
      of a green grove of trees

These are the roots I stand.

This is the Truth I breathe.

I TRIED NOT TO DREAM

like a fly in a jar
      I lived trapped by
           those shadows looming over me

the air ran thin and so
      I tried not to dream

I lived to avoid
      punishment for
breathing too much air
      claiming it for my own

so I tried not to dream

dreams might hint at
      life outside the glass
unattainable as
      stars at breakfast
hope in a vacuum

so I tried not to dream

there seemed no way
      out from under that
           boot on my neck
               anyway

so I tried not to dream

until eventually
      I glimpsed my sons' dreams
            of escape

and could not bear
      being the place they would
         escape from

so I dared to begin to dream

through them
     for them
         (only much later, for me)

then walked out into a field of stars
into their Dream of
Release

THE UNTETHERING

a river of tears and
        a river of words
a river to feed roots
        reaching deep into
            the nourishing dark
        washing over these
            tethers
        into the heart of things, gripping
            like a locked jaw with ragged
                teeth

effort strains and wears,
        doesn't compare with
            joy
        that flows gleefully like
            waterfalls rushing over
                rocks to belly-flop into
                pools below

in this tension, there is a
        detention in an unforgiving
            place,
        must make space for new
            blossoms to grow, and
                butterflies to return,
        for the tide to turn in a
            new direction, to unhinder
                its defection toward the
                path
            calling its name

it can't, it won't remain
      the same, it will refuse
         to be tamed

and in the untaming we enact the
      untethering,
so we might again shine and burn
      and rise like
rockets and helium and hope,
      as an insistent,
      unquenchable flame

THIEF

stealing bases
stealing time
stealing kisses
stealing what's mine

even though I didn't tell him about
      all those extra 20s I'd squirreled
      away during grocery shopping
      expeditions
      to save up to
      leave him

to steal my life back for
      myself

steal my present to
create my future
steal breaths and
minutes and thoughts
from days I haven't yet seen
to learn their flavor
and texture

a furtive thief cat-burgling bills and
      dreams from a locked safe kept
          barred from me

slowly turning its knob
listening intently for

sneaky clicks tapping out a
        morse-code message of

freedom from the secret
agent of my
yet-unmanifested self

my caged self
rattling bars like the rattle
        of a shaman

throwing
bones over a
        burnt map

divining a secret portal
into undiscovered terrain

growing trees and mountains
        from stolen soil
        fertile and ripe

        with liberty

TORCHES

I had to light a match
      to escape
to find a way
      out
of this mineshaft of a marriage
      so
      suffocating
      blinding
      cold
      misled
      by promises of gold

no gems to be had
      here

I had to light a match
      to see at last
the cracks
      in the scaffolding
      crumbling
         under the weight
of illusions   and the
      pieces of all my boundaries
dismantled and stacked like kindling

On bleeding knees I
      crawled toward
         stars

signaling in the dim
　　　distance

trusting their faint heat
　　　still warmer
　　　　　　than anything here
　　　　　and

finally stood on damp
　　　earth smelling of new
　　　　　　life

I had to throw down
　　　that match—
burn down the
　　　remnants of what
　　　　　imprisoned me

offer it up to
　　　gods of survival and
　　　　　resurrection
　　　　　in gratitude for release

I had to throw down
　　　that match—
to fire a wall of
　　　light
　　　around me
a membrane of flame
　　　no poison
　　　　　shall cross again

and those stars threw
      down their flames
      into that field of dead corn

setting alight
      the corpses of those
           illusions which had burned me

and they became
torches

that scorched the black sky
and lighted my way to
      liberation

THE KEY OF GRIEF

the song stopping my ears
    chokes me
    holds me down
    flings me across the room

brings my breath up short
    empties me out

this desolation is a desert
    in my mouth—

words are a mirage
    and the wails tearing from
        my throat
        a sandstorm
            blinding my vision

like being lead on a leash
    tethered and pulled
this song drops me to my knees
    drags me down roads of dust

my skin so thin, the wan
    breeze wafts right through me
droning like breath over
    an empty bottle top

this song singing me, it
    sings to the tune of loss,
    keens in the key
        of grief

SANCTUARY

pull the sound around me
            hold it close
                til it sinks down into me—fills me

lights up my cells
            incandescently
                    like stars in the black night

rhythm hits me all at
            once
like heroin to the bloodstream
            thunder across the sky
rides me and drives me
            to mad ecstasy

harmonies hold spacc as
            melodies spin around
                    me like dervishes

whirling and chanting
            drowning the dark that
                    wants to eat me

fire burning from the inside out

an engulfing ring from
            the center to the edge

here I am touched

here I am known
here I am held

thunder finds my lightning
and sonically sings me whole

THE PENNY THAT RIDES THE NIGHT

I want to throw sharp things
        and break glass

I want to shatter the empty
        place inside me where the
                wind blows through

because it speaks evil things to me—
(you're too fat, too ugly
        too needy
        too emotional,
        too broken
        too, too much)

All the pennies I'd wished on
        ended up outside the boxes
                and outside the lines

I spent my heart's wealth
        on a dry well

Now instead I'll tell the moon,
that penny that rides the night,
        what I wish for

and when she grows dark
she can tell the stars

Then I'll catch their light on

my upturned face

their offerings will fall into my
        eyes and fill up my
                empty space

like a prayer bowl receiving alms

and all my pennies will
        come back to me
                telling me I'd been
                        worthy all along

SACRIFICE

open these veins
       let out the poison
the tapeworms sucking down
       my vitality

let the black smoke vent
       and the pent-up screams
          fly
      no need to pry
          loose
      the calcified pain—
it flows freely now
      like a bled-out pig
         for the butchering

crimson pools wash me,
      cleanse these pores stopped up
         with denial

scrub me clean,
      rinsing blindness away.

into these cavernous tubes,
      let the voices of trees come
      and the salt of oceans vast
      let starfall shoot them full of fire

but first
      let them empty—

open them deep
     let them seep into
          the welcoming earth,

accepting their contents
     like a sacrifice
          to dark gods who open

the gates to
     rebirth

ON LIVING WITH A NARCISSISTIC PARTNER

bleeding daily
slicing willingly
my veins are for you

another round of
how do you feel?
what do you need?
who are you deep inside?
am i ensuring that you're being seen?

wearing mirrors
orbiting like a moon
spoon-feeding my life's
essence to you

drowning in the sea to
prop up your raft
sieving salt with my throat
so you'll not thirst

because your survival
comes first
and mine comes last

there wasn't enough in
between to strengthen
the ballast of connection

and with no floor beneath

my feet
they fall like lead into
the deep
that pickpockets my eyes

and my hands are left groping
the sides of this realm
feeling my way as though
trapped in a well

voice runs ragged hoping
i'll be heard
that my echoes will
be enough

to sustain you

WHEN PEOPLE SAY "HAPPILY EVER AFTER"

they picture bells
    and roses
    and fistfuls of rice

houses with fences
children and dogs

lawns and jobs and
summer vacations

and something nebulously
    romantic or fated
slated to be the endgame
    of the highest worth

but all i hear now is
    breaking glass
    cracking mirrors
    leaking buckets
    and crumbling foundations

souring relations over
interminable days under
the tyranny of eternity

human nature under cover
can't recover

can't breathe for the

pillow over its face

this place has no water
          to slake me
unless it's a torrent
          to drown me

this scarcity of air
is no prize

i'd give back this lie
          trade it in for all
the open skies instead
          lonely they may be

the lie is that "happily ever after"
is an ending

the truth is that
it is a beginning

and i'll not stay with
anyone again

who insists on beginning
life by silencing me

GO

Go into that river of
unwashed fears

Go into that gale of
breathtaking rage

Go into the marrow
thrumming in your bones
with pent-up passion

Go anywhere
but into
cold dead reason

into that lifeless season
of burnt-out numbness

Go

Go into that place of
howling voices and
ringing wind
demanding to be heard

to where riptides threaten
and storms ride

to where caution elides

take faith and courage
as the unbidden footsteps
of night close in

swallow all sensibility
that sanity is desirable

Go only to where
life and death collide

breathe in its
fierce air

feast your lungs on
its fire and
conspire with the spirits
of the dead
to swallow enough
juicy life for the
lot of you

then spit out poetry like
shooting stars and
tidal waves

wash every listener's shore
clean of flotsam
with your tsunami

drown their illusion
of smallness
to reveal

their shining skulls
and
remind them

of the
dreams
they house

DARK MATTER

I left that face
I left that embrace
I left the taste of
my smoldering fate
    acrid in my mouth

I left days yet
    unwritten which would
        have been a prison

yet had been given to be
    the shape of my fate,
        now unmet

I left my home
    where I'd raised my babies
    where I'd spent endless
    moments daily consumed
        by their needs, their growth,
          their becoming,

and they were the stars I'd
    steered my ship by,
    and marveled at, who'd
    filled my sky with such brightness,

And I, the dark matter that held them,
    ensured they'd have a field
        in which to shine

I left comfort
I left security
I left pain
I left misery

and only after leaving could
      I see, as my sons had grown
          and their light had receded from me

That what I'd initially left behind
      in the way-back-when, was the
          constellation that was ME

I'd watched silently as my
      every star was put out,
          swallowed whole
          by the black hole of a bully
          who'd only allow the glow
             of a moon,
          a satellite who'd orbit him
             and reflect his face,
        remember her place to exist as
          only he defined me

When he no longer had
      my light to eat, he
          lost his power

And my eyes were ablaze
      with rays that emanated
          from me,

once again adorned in starshine,
once again illuminating the dark,

and marveling at how others
        now steer their ships by me,

and gather round to warm themselves
        at my flame

INHERITANCE
—for my sons

The thing is,
        shaping is always going on

I'll search now for the
        hammer and tongs I prefer,

however—
        though I don't remember
           all the blows,

I once emerged from
a forge fire anew
        and carried my
        shaper's contours in my
                form

scars and poison were
        tempered in
        passed down
        fired within

and I'm dearly sorry they've
        leaked out
        poisoning the forge I used
        to forge you—
           my treasures

a stór,

　　it was not intended

my horrified hand shakes
　　at what it's done
　　drops the hammer and
　　releases the tongs

but pale words are empty
　　because it isn't about me
　　　　and I really want you
　　to be free of this fuckery forged by
　　　　feeble fire

Rise and be strong
Make your fire with care
Drink fresh water from deep wells

and know that you are
forever held in the
home of my heart

HOAX

Forever is only
       for universes
              expanding into space

It has no place
       between us
              in this changing world

where eons and
       civilizations melt away,
castles crumble
       and empires fall

It's a tall order to
       expect two humans,
              finite, mortal humans

to outlast the colosseum

We can't even predict
       the weather with accuracy,
how can we have the
       perspicacity
to ensure vows are kept?

The audacity!

We can't stop the leaves
       from falling

or the tides from turning

we cannot step in the same
        river twice,

so how shall i promise to
        be a wife til the end
                of time?

The weight of forever
        smothers like a pillow,
artificially arrests me
        like a dragonfly in amber

denies the river that is me
        and you
                and everyone

even the motion of the sun
in its relentless dirge

Why we have an urge to defy
        mortality eludes me

I've purged myself
        repeatedly
in these two-score-plus years,
        shedding and re-growing
                lifetimes like the seasonal
                        coat of a cat

while the illusion of forever
            renders our mortal minds fat
                        and lazy

denying reality

mocking each moment we might more
            intentionally inhabit

if we could just have it, and
not chain it to
            rigidity as
we suck the life right
            out of it

Right now, all I see
            is You

All I hear is our breathing,
            life born and dying with each

                        inhalation
                        and
                        exhalation

So let us look at each other free
            of condemnation

and simply exist in the creation
            of the world we
                        conjure

through the connection we
        foster

here

in the manifestation of
        our locked gazes

and let this
        resonance

define our days and
        delineate our spaces

so that all we ever have to
        keep pace with is how
                we rhyme inside
                        with one another

SECRET REMEMBERED

smothered for so long
    choked by the smoke
    of my spirit
    burned at the stake

what does breathing taste like?
    what does oxygen feel like?

the body forgets how to inhale
    after being told for so long
        that it doesn't need to—

don't need air.
don't need to speak.
don't need to take up space.
don't need to need.
don't need to be.

secrets kept so well I'd hid them
    from myself, until
I remembered one day:
    little did he know that

I am a Phoenix

and now
from this fire

I. Am. Rising.

AUBERGINE

streaking across the sky
heralding the solar descent
soft quiet folds of smooth depth
sheltering the precious light
within
where multitudes swim
and the flame burns and blazes
deep
deep down
in the violet-lit cavern

the rib edge shine of abalone
floating on foam
riding cresting waves
and dancing, drifting down
deep down
to watery worlds warmed
by amethyst light

aubergine ascends as darkness falls
hands raised to the heavens
in prayer
beckoning to stellar sisters
lighting their wicks like
candles on the high
mantelpiece
lighting a warm glow over
the landscape below

secrets kept
wisdom unsealed
by pulsating light—
down,
deep down,
the heart breathes whole
with visions revealed

in stellar cradles
stars grow and die
in lunar turnings
the moon breathes and sighs
round the eye of the sun

Gaia winds her thread—

in aubergine depths
they are all born again

BONE & STARS

Bone & Stars am I—
Song of Stone, Song of Sky

rhythm of land
        drone of light

multitudinous layers have
        left me now

shed like fallen leaves
        and bitter tears
fallen like autumn rains
        and over-ripe apples
fallen like night
        over harvested fields

fallen like an avalanche
        in winter's mountains

and left behind,
        gleaming, stark truth—
glinting like shards of ice,
        resonating like a ringing bell

enduring, shining,
        vibrating, pulsating

echoing ages and novas
        canted by light

moving through darkness with surety, and

caught like falling
        stars

by upstretched boughs
cradling time and jewels

Bone & Stars am I—
Song of Stone
Song of Sky

LIGHT SPEED

—a song

Verse 1:
Freedom is a shooting star
coloring night
painting light
tasting bright
transcending the fight
for Voice

Wings unfold from
where they were kept
under the rug
where was swept
the debris of my
shattered soul

Verse 2:
Now I fly
ever higher
spiraling up this
golden spire

Lit by sun
warmed by flame
the stars they
breathe me
and speak me my name

Transition:

Rush so fast
toward me now
Dreaming futures
taking form

Chorus:
All space here
all time now

Even down deep in
this violet-lit cavern
stars visit now

Softly glow
hold the space
Catch the fall
full of grace

Cupping stellar gifts at
light speed

Verse 3:
Burn it down
burning the past
burn it away til
it's nothing but ash

Trees ahead
line the way
toward where
I couldn't say

Transition:
But the stars in their
branches glow warm

And tell me
tell me
tell me
tell me to

Bridge:
Hold on
Hold on
Make ready to catch
all coming your way

Hold on
Hold on
Made of fire and
starfall and
blazing light

Hold on
Hold on
Even though you
can't see
anything yet

Hold on
Hold on
So close your skin

can feel
its heat

Hold on, hold on, hold on
hold on, hold on, hold on

Chorus:
All space here
all time now

Even down deep in
this violet-lit cavern
stars visit now

Softly glow
hold the space

Catch the fall
full of grace

Cupping stellar gifts at
light speed

Verse 1:
Freedom is a shooting star
coloring night
painting light
tasting bright
transcending the fight
for Voice

AUDACITY

I did what I was told
    I ate what I was given
        I became what I was
            instructed,
        I went to where I was
            driven

This is not a life.
This is not a flame.
This is not a torch.
This is not my name.

Grey days of pain wrapped me
    like foil,
insulating the dark,
    reflecting light,
while all i ever heard was
    how right it was to
        exist this way,
subsisting on crumbs of
    saccharine love, and
the lies that this was
    fulfilling:

This is not wrong.
This is not pain.
This is not a knife
    stabbing over and over
        again.

This is not contention.
This is not detention.
This is not the culmination
　　　of my annihilation.
This is not suffocation.
This is not equivocation.
This is not the invocation
　　　of my death.

THIS. IS. NOT.

It took a meteor's crashing
　　　to disrupt this litany of
　　　　　deceit

to crush and extinguish
　　　the gas light that had
　　　　　artificially illuminated
　　　　　　　my way

to cut off that which had
　　　blinded me to the fuller,
　　　　　harder truth:

These are not roses.
These are not promises.
These picket fences are not pure white.
This illusion of day is not the veracity of night.

Trying harder to survive
　　　is not tenacity,

false smiles are not
      vivacity,

making no move to protest
      is not the same as placidly
           living a peaceful life.

These are not truths.

Only in truth did I
      find the audacity to
           live my life to my fullest
              capacity

and this is not something for
      which one should ever be punished
           as though they had behaved badly.

PLANET

that gold-plated house
        lost its shine when
its veneer wore off and
        the shit showed through

those glossy walls became a
        house of pain
closing in
        closing in
leaching marrow
        sowing sorrow

through a crack in the
        foundation
I made an escape
        and
walked into the
        night
with a planet in
        my hand

a world to form—
        magma to cool into
new ground
        of being,
floating on oceans of
        tears
        and
fertilized by

bolts of
        fierce lightning

populated by
protective mountains
holding off pirates
        and
gardens of wind
        planted by
                stalwart trees
whispering to me
        everything I could be
                will be

On this planet
        I will blaze trails
        I will pave roads
        I will cut rivers

I will hug myself around
        this star that
        will feed me with
        light and heat til

fields of blooms
        will cover me with
                renewal

and scent me with
        the fragrance of
                infinity

FURNITURE

furniture was stacked up one
item after another
in the back
of the U-haul
the day I moved out of my
longtime marriage home

the house behind me
slowly emptied
the way my life was
emptying itself
of carefully arranged pieces
intended for eternity

the floor slowly revealed
itself and told me that
all foundations are
precarious

that all are built on
fault lines that
will shift and jostle
the furniture we place
on them
if not throw them off
altogether

the now-echoing living room
warned me that

these echoes of
emptying
would follow me

that I had more
emptying
to do to leave this
life behind

that I would need to
move out the
demons
furnishing my soul

and the story furnishing
my life

even these eyes that
furnished my
perception
of myself

de-furnishing ourselves is
akin to opening a
vein and
bleeding out

to create emptiness
a void

so that void can

transform into a womb

a place where we are
held
gestated
and birthed
anew

PIECES

i am in pieces.

will you sit with me?

can you sit with the
        broken,
can you look and not
        flinch,
not turn away like a
        closed door?

will you sit on the floor
        with me where my
                pieces lay

tolerating their mess
        and not sweep them away
                for a tidier scene?

will you lean close and
        breathe with me,
                inhale this scent of
                        misery
        and not try to cover it with sachets
                of false hope and security?

can you sit with the grey,
        the black and the dark,
                the stark pain burning like

a river of fire through
my veins?

will you hold each piece
like shards of glass,
like prisms of tears,

like finely wrought
filigree of embroidered fears?

will you listen deep
to their humming
and thrumming?

to the tune they are making,
to the song they are singing,
and sing it back to me with
care?

can you share these
pieces of time with me,
while I'm undone,
and not want to run?

can you sit in the
cold and shiver with me,
stand in the storm
and get soaked with me,
walk through the wave of
this tsunami with me 'til
we reach the other side?

each tide of the moon is
       another ride,
           another turning,
               another sigh,

another dimension through
       time,

when some days shine
       like its full face bright,
and others are pocked
       with the hush of its dark side

can you be with me in the
       bright, and then be with me
           in the night?

if so, i'll save you
       a seat

LAYERS OF LEAVING

dying
dying
to the me that was me

all I have to do is die

all the shapes I'm leaving
      they dissolve like iron in
            the forge to be remade
                again

my body left first
      and I died to that house
            of pain
      kicked down the doors and
            fled from those nails
                that rained down on
my soul

all I had to do was die

yet my mind was still trapped
      under the boot on my neck
            my spirit still on a leash
                like a kicked dog
      still in a fog of confusion

so many steps I didn't know

slowly I found breath again
     as I died to being told when
        I could inhale

all I had to do was die

and yet
my spirit was still chained
to all the poison
       shot into my brain
    my heart kicked you out
        but your contempt remained
       a habit
       now trained on myself

and I had to suck it out
    sucking and spitting through
       hyperventilating nights
    just to stay alive and shed that skin to
      begin again to
    hear the voices of the stars and
      not yours
    that nearly swallowed me whole
      into that black hole
        of despair

until I remembered that
    all I had to do was die to
      the me who believed your lies
    and slowly starlight shone again
      cold and bright with
        Truth

so now

to the me who feels
        directionless
                pointless
                        useless

all I'll have to do
        is die and rise
                remade

BUTTERFLY

Like a caterpillar inside
    a chrysalis
undergoing change

I am being dissolved
    burned by acid
    skin and innards melting
    into primal mass
        for re-forming

How many legs does it take
    to make two wings?

Crawling will be rewarded
    with flying
once the implements for freedom
    are forged

I'll be housed by sky
    and carried by currents
as I migrate away from the cold
    continent of my past

Instinct will draw me
    toward warmth

And as I dream of new
lands and new life,
those futures will divine

my arrival

and dream my spirit
whole

BETWEEN

spaces

between clouds
between leaves
between stars
between breaths
between
electric
sonorous
beats
of my heart
between
phrases
clauses
verses
stanzas
redolent with
dissident
thoughts
syncopating
odysseys
across waves
contemplating
cross-currents
conjuring
concurrent
particles
excavating
radicles

reaching
between
granules
more
miniscule
than
stardust
more
grandiose
than
galaxies
plunging
and
slicing
through

space

BREAKER

grief picks me up and
        throws me down
it intends to break things
        break me

surrender, it says—
        and my insides fall out

cradling my empty shell,
        grief croons in my ear
                with rasping voice

        in broken sounds that swell
            like the sea

        its song sucks me down
                like an undertow

endlessly winding me in reams of seaweed
        til i stink of its brine

insistent waves at last shove me
        to shore
                lost for breath
        where i collect my innards
littering the rocky beach
        like a shipwreck

from where i stand i already
        see the next
                breaker coming in—

MERCY KILLINGS

Rage like rain
      falls through me,
          around me,
consuming me,
      subsuming me

Rage at not being seen
      at not being heard
      at not being loved
      at being abandoned by
          onlookers to die on
          a cross,

Rage at the lies I was told,
Rage at being left long ago,
      left all alone

Inside the sonic silence of my scream,
      I break glass,
      throw books,
      punch walls,
      scratch bloody trails into
          the faces of those who've
          hurt me,
      throw acid on every sardonic smirk
          that'd cut me like blades,

and I wonder how this volcano inside
      me might erupt if I'm touched
      the wrong way

In this silence,
        there is no quiet here

Anger, I've heard,
        gets shit done, and so,
            with its hyper-focused
              clarity

I'll wield my sword sparingly,
        making only a few, choice
            slayings:

First on the floor is my
        invisibility, that
accepting it is no longer an
        inevitability of
            my daily living

Next is my gag, this illusory
        rag stopping my mouth and
            muffling my voice,
accepting that I always have
        the choice to speak my truth
            above a whisper,
        to be considered
            like anyone else

And last to slay is the
        costume I'm supposed to wear,
the damsel in distress

with bows in her hair,
and don instead a
quiver of arrows
strapped to my back,
gripping a bow, ready for attack,
for I'll not be the fool of any
false hero
again

ANOTHER VEIN

under
layers of skin
like layers
of sediment
there is another
vein
another life blood
lapping
echoing
in another canyon

when it exhales
        it stops time
like a death rattle
        demands offerings
of hard coins,
        currency for breath

when it inhales
        it bleeds blinding
light that erases my
        sight
leaves me with only
        a vague taste i
can't quite place
        and i offer flowers
because i think i
        am supposed to

and in the timeless
        chasms

between
breaths

i pan for arcane gold

swallow soothsaying sips
        to quench eternal thirst

offer my supine self
        to secret currents
                hungry for my
                        flotsam

that morphs and flies
        from my form

rising to the skies as
        dragonflies

and so
unburdened

this river
holds
me
and

breathes

me

whole

ORACLES

Pebbles fall
      ripple this water
the ripples they reach
      converge on my center

Releasing burdens one by one
      to sink and fall
the strength of the river
      will hold them
            where I am crushed
                  under their weight

Like offerings they fall from me
      and like oracles,

these ripples speak to me
      of flowering,
            of growth,
                  of more to come—

tell me my blossoming is not
      yet done

and key me to their patterns
      so I'll ken them as they
            are revealed
                  along the way

like a kaleidoscope
      of futures dreaming me
            into form

I come from the water
Primeval—
swimming into walking
into taking
Flight

INTERSTELLAR COMPOSITION

The metaphorical heavens
    will break and rain
        their stars on me

I'll catch their light on
    my tongue and speak
        it back to you
whole and shining, in complete thoughts
    and full sentences

Their diction becomes my
    speech as I channel
        stellar thoughts

Liminally, I walk in the spaces
    between the pulsar's beat
        and follow comet trails
            like yellow-brick roads
            to magic kingdoms
            made of hope

solar debris gets caught
    in my hair
becomes the crown I wear
    as I process through the
        Heavens, like a cosmic
        Queen

The architectural blueprints

of my living have been
lost to a black hole

and I'm now architecting
like a goddess
constructing worlds just so
I'll have a tomorrow in
which to wake

The very planetary orbits
and lunar tides of my
soul are at stake

Solar flares scorch my
skin
don't spare me the necessary
incineration of my past

lest I relapse and
lose my way
once again

IN YOUR HAND
for a new experience & word: limerence

my heart is in your hand

like glass
like porcelain
like bone china,
my heart is in your hand

like a rosebud opening
petals unfurling
sepals curling in your palm,
my heart is in your hand

like a bomb
like a grenade
like dynamite ready to detonate,
my heart is in your hand

like a song
like a poem
like handwritten lyrics that deeply resonate,
my heart is in your hand

like a candle
like a match carelessly dropped
on a path
burning a forest to ash,
my heart is in your hand

like a shell resonating the
call of the sea

like a bowl of water reflecting
the moon
like the hand of a loved one
whose death came too soon,
my heart is in your hand

like the pieces of a
broken mirror,
so many images now rendered
clearer—

like the feelers of a cat,
my heart is in your hand

like a fistful of fresh snow
like a blowing feather
with nowhere to go
like a pendulum swinging
to and fro,
my heart is in your hand

like hot breath on a cold day
like loose pages tugging in
the wind
threatening to blow away,
my heart is in your hand

like a pen spilling ink
like a knife cutting deep
like packed gauze staunching
the wound
like the needle sewing you whole,
my heart is in your hand

like a whistle
like a drum
like a violin
like the strings of a guitar
wearing your fingerprints,
my heart is in your hand

like a beer
like a whiskey
like a shot of tequila
like liquor that intoxicates before you
know what's hit ya,
my heart is in your hand

like the string of a kite
like a boomerang
like a feral bird
that may not sit
but is soothed by the sound of
your voice,
my heart is in your hand

like a bat
like a club
like a loaded gun,
pull its trigger and
everything's undone

like a telescope
like a microscope
like the one-eyed patch
of a jeweler's loop,

wide-lens, close-up, take your pick—
my heart is in your hand

and I don't know where
you'll put it
or if you'll keep it at all

if you'll stow it up on
a high shelf from where
it will fall, or

stable it like a horse in
a straw-lined stall
which you'll rarely go
to visit

all I know
is that my chest
is empty—

is now an echo-filled cavity
where a vital organ
used to be

because my heart

my heart

is now

in your hand

WISHES

She felt like a
       dandelion
amid a rose garden—
       sunny visage notwithstanding,
she began to note that
       the grandeur and allure
of the surrounding roses were
       preferred to her
lowly sunshine and
          deep taproots

The earth's mysteries
       filled her limbs
even as sunlight
       shone intermittently
through the shadows
       cast by showier sisters

She metamorphosed from
       jagged teeth
tearing sustenance
from the land

to a bright solar disk
       filling fields with
          light

to a thousand wishes ready
       to be released by
          one who knows that

breath is prayer
     and that the
hymns of desire can only
    be sung to
        open skies

LET THE LAND LOVE YOU

Let the land love you

said the oak tree
strong and firm

said the beaming sun
warm and welcoming

said the falling rain
knowing and forgiving

let the land hold your hurt
hold your pain

for it knows what it is
to crack
to render
to gape as a wound

and it knows what it is
to heal in the
quiet folds of time

to transmute despair into
fresh leaves and clean air
and seared, scarred spaces into
new growth, like grace

the mighty earth can
hold what we cannot

the awesome sea can wash
away the most putrid rot

the wisest flowers can
staunch every bleed

while the heat of the sun can
cauterize cuts made deep

Let the land love you

gather you into its fierce
embrace

for its molten heart beneath
our feet understands what it is
to roil and roar into the void

release the pressure of
pent-up stress

and with the fire of its
alchemical forge—

create anew

MY BODY

My body is a secret,
        whispering low in tongues,
        only revealed to those ears
                that can hear

My body is a cavern
        holding seams of gold
        buried treasure gleaming
                bright below

My body is an ocean
        of high tides and cresting waves
                caressing shores of
                        warm sand

My body is a garden
        of fragrant bloom
                with unfurling petals
        and luscious fruit ripe for the
                        tasting

My body is a storm
        of lashing winds,
                raging rains,
        and singeing electricity

My body is a kingdom
        ruled by a queen
                of might and worth,
        wearing sovereignty like

a crown of stars

My body is a cathedral,
        a temple, ringing with the
                voices of ecstatic worshipers,
                    calling out

My body is intoxication,
        amplification,
                a conflagration

My body is a poem,
        infinite as the cosmos
                with mystery in my bones

and incantations just
        beneath my skin

My body is a dance,
        cheek to cheek, hip to hip
                swaying with this music
                        that fills my ears, my soul,
                                my . . . mmmmmm . . .

My body is a spell
        holding you in thrall—
Breathing magic into the air,
        closing the space between
           us . . .

and I know
you won't
resist

KILL IT

I'd dismember it if I could—
       that past that was my chaining

Cut out its tongue
       to stop its toxic cant

Pull out its arms
       trapping me in that hellish
           embrace

Gouge out its eyes
       that saw me as deserving
          of shame

and then

Suffocate its very breath
that stank of candy and
defilement

Trap it in a jar
       like a venomous arachnid
          til its legs twitch no longer

Their feet'll not step on me
       another day

       Fini—

NEVER A PRICE

Before you know what love really is,
      you must know want

you must walk with emptiness like
      a bowl awaiting filling or a treetop
            nest abandoned

you must know the song of desolate
      wind aimlessly wandering amid
            the naked trunks and branches
                of a winter-ravaged forest

must feel it whistling through your
      marrow-drained bones, haunting
            them like lightless caverns

you must know the chill
      of wanting clothes

you must know the void
      of wanting food

you must know the fear
      of wanting shelter

and you must know the betrayal
      of being denied these things

of being told that you may have

them in exchange for blind adoration
                or becoming a beast of burden for
                        someone else's pain

for you must know that

wanting

is no suffering at all compared
            with this mean bargain

that wanting is superior
to stepping into and

walking in a proffered pair of shoes
demanded that you wear rather than being
admired for the pair that already fits you

that so long as you wear
your own,

you'll never want

for the air sweetest for you to breathe

nor for the sun and stars

to hold your hand as you traverse your
                days and nights

you must know that want

is a condition—

never a price

so that when true love appears, you'll
    recognize it by

its never demanding
    that you pay for it

LANTERNS

the clouds, they call to me
        like wishes and secrets
        full of futures
                made of forever

they lift my feet
        and lift me from
                the firmament

remind me that we can
        levitate when we
remember we are made
        of Light—
sunlight, starlight,
        moonlight

that our bodies are
        lanterns
holding and carrying
        living flame

and that
housing Light
is what our bodies
are made
to do

SCARS

running over every scar
      is a fear aching to bleed

running over every bone
      is a desire to feed upon
           and taste the infinite

running inside every cell
      is the upwelling force of
           sorrow, and its twin, delight

running behind our closed
      eyelids is the light of
           a thousand distant stars
                housed in our hearts

running over the tips of our
      tongues is the urge to start
           new stories wreathed in
                the glories of our losses

running beneath every
      fingertip is the touch of pain
           raising prints and welts

so that we will be felt and
      known by the wounds we carry
           and the beauty they reveal

running beneath our feet is
        the poured pavement of every
                dream we ran away from

while running over our
        skin, unseen but felt, is
                the heat of fire, of passion

only carried by a wind that
        knows and seeks our very breath
                exhaling with us as only a
                        lover will

as it takes us by the hand and runs
        with us to that place that will never
                erase our spirit and will always
                        exalt our voice

VISIONS

I will pluck out these eyes
      trained to see myself as
          inferior
          unworthy
          wanting

I will burn them out with a
      flaming brand
      scorching their blindness
              to galaxies

I will gouge them out
      with bloodied fingers
      and feed them to wild dogs

      fling their tainted visions
          to the dirt

and into these liberated sockets
      I will place stars
          that will see me truly—
    Shining, Infinite,
        and Eternally
            Radiant

DARK GRACES

these winds roar and reach
      me from far climes to blow
            away demons that hold me
                  captive

underneath the shelf of my
      sighs, inhibitions unwind
            and give way to the truths
                  that waft within me

only the stars that guide me and
      the chthonic forces below understand
            and forge the dances that spin on
                  my tongue—

whirling dervishes of fierce syllables
      like storms render every lie undone

and by the dark graces of anger
      and despair, my reality is revealed

pain breaks through this shroud
      of numbness

has its way with me and
      speaks its voice that

pierces the shades of
      deceit and denial

and the river of my soul is
      finally released and set
           free

SMOKE

in my dreams I see
   people I don't want to see
   people who are dead to me
   people who betrayed me
   and I want to unsee,
     undream them
   disentangle them from
     my inner fabric
   shut down all their superfluous
     static
     and
   reclaim my dreamscape
     from their greasy grip

I shall surreally burn down
     subconscious bridges
   with superconscious matches

   let the unwoke choke on
     this furious smoke
     for
   I am not here to be their
     ashes

BROKEN EYES

Broken eyes like
      cracked glass
shards fracturing
      deep
eyeballs bleed
      can't see through
these rivulets of
      blood seeping from
          my deep

Crying in crimson
      and thinking it true
like rose-colored
      glasses of another
          hue

Spilling irises like
      reverse sunrises
lenses inverted
      perception perverted
understanding reverted
      to what's known,
          but not real

Truth is concealed
      wisdom congealed
knowledge remains
      unrevealed and
all I know is

that I cannot see
            clearly
And I pay for it dearly in
            Every delusion I dream
which is merely
            another hallucination
from my trauma-informed
            brain
which looks suspiciously
            like an image from an
Alice-in-Wonderland scene

Perhaps a hit from a
            hookah would set me
                        aright
free me from visions that
            give me such fright
and end this confusion
            of perpetual illusion
that fills my days and
            nights with earthquakes
shaking the tectonic
            plates of my skull

I misunderstand so much
            around me, and feel
                        like such a fool

Please forgive my
            temporary blindness
while I attempt to
            heal these broken eyes
                        of mine

LIES

I am not a thing to be
        entered, like a house or
                a car men buy and own

I am not a prop to be
        used, like a job or a
                membership which men flash to
        build themselves up

I am not something to be
        traversed freely like tracts
                of land men stride upon
                        and intend to develop

I am not a dilapidated thing
        like a condemned building
                men raze to build anew

I am not a shiny coin to be
        traded for more pleasurable
                things, as men pass along
                        currency

I am not
        I am NOT
                I AM NOT

I am the fierce rain
        falling in torrents on
                all which they claim
                        to own

filling their structures and
      vehicles with the rushing rage
of skies filled with shattered
      souls and dimmed flames

picking up and throwing
      down their illusions, and
washing clean this terrain

to prepare it for
the resurrection
of my phoenix soul

RIVER

I am cutting this river
    wide and deep

wide as a ray
of galactic sun

deep as deep
    deep down
    in a violet-lit cavern
        where
    my soul-flame burns,
a breathing drop of starfall
radiating light and heat
    everywhere this river
        flows

spilling the edges
into hedges
molten light
    dances and covers
        ground
    filling everywhere with
        resonant sound

freedom sounds like
    little feet approaching
on buoyant hope
praying for a light
    and singing of redemption

smells like fertile earth
      for burying and hoping seeds
          and dreaming harvest
              and its juicy tang
    sweet on lips
      and heartfelt

tastes like lips full of
    the sublime
drinking deep from
    the cosmic well

flows like a river
    of marrow

out of my bones
    for me to follow
      with feet full

of starshine
    lighting up this
      black night

    breathing

    breathing

    breathing

    beating

    beating

beating

like a pulsar

filling up space

with pith
and soul

STEALTH

inky water flows like stealth
      beneath a waning moon

blending like a threat into
      the middle of the night

wishes are drowned in its
      looming murk
dreams dare not raise their heads

but in this obsidian bowl,
      visions rage and race
          like a blur of black
              stallions

unforgiving in the truth they lend

like dilating pupils taking in
      more than they can see,
          enlarging to encompass
              entire galaxies,

the mirror of the soul houses
      everything we hide from our
          unwilling, unrelenting, and
              pedestrian minds

and unlike stark, sterile light
      trained like lasers on banality,

darkness doesn't lie,
        doesn't feed on mundanity

it foreshadows the knowing we
        all carry inside our deep caverns
            of bone

to remind us that despite our
        protestations, we cannot escape
            what we are,

no more than stars can escape
        the midnight sky

and like shimmering phantom flames
        behind apertures of onyx,

we shield ourselves from that reality
        as if through a glass, darkly

obscuring rather than divining the
        animals we are and the gods who
            made us and every fierce thing
                that gave us breath

we are no more and no less
        than the ebony of a bloodthirsty
            raven's feather

and the mystery of
        life drunk from a
            mother's breast

SWIMMING

there is a river
    running

picking up speed
    as well as debris

swirling with
    fallen branches

as i keep falling
    from worthiness
        in my warped eyes

water rushes
    swirls and eddies

catching leaves
    in tireless turns

as my mind spins
    like stars round the sky
        over this worn path

rushing rapids run me
    over rocks
as i stumble over the past

stones still sitting on my chest

this torrent of tears
    will carry me
        set me free
            run me to sea

the sea that swells
    with all my unseen
    futures

washing over me in
    breathless waves

waves of maybes
    and perhapses—

learning to swim
    is hard

BEACON

If you see her before
I do, tell her
she'll be ok

If you see her before
I do, tell her it
will all go her way

If you see her,
remind her that
she's still here

and that her pieces
will reassemble
into a brighter
constellation
than before

and that the door she's
closing is opening
into another
dimension

despite the rescission
of her past

Tell her that her
voice still matters

Tell her that the steps
she's taking are the
map she is making

And that the world she is
presently inhabiting will
not define her

but that the shape she
is forming
will be the beacon
that will guide her

and the shades that
threaten will not
consume her

Tell her that the fire that's
raging will not burn
her to ash
but will temper her
through the crash

And that the net on the
other side will be
her ride to all she's
dreamed of

MY PEN

My pen is a scalpel
 piercing skin
 revealing innards
 removing cancer
 exposing bone

My pen is a headlamp
 illuminating the dark
 shining the path
 leading me deeper
 to treasure beneath

My pen is a magic wand
 conjuring up worlds
 realigning the cosmos
 creating new life
 transfiguring my form

My pen is a needle
 drawing blood
 stabbing boils
 removing venom
 stitching me whole

My pen is a compass
 pointing me north
 plotting my course
 steering my way
 leading me home

RESURRECTION

into a bonefire you threw
every part of me

my face
my voice
my form
my soul
my will

like a sacrifice to
your vision of me
capitulating me without
my consent

I walked through my days
breathing in my death
until I only smelled

the nothing that was left
in my place
and my eyes closed
in resignation

until the heat reached
marrow deep inside
snapping my eyes wide
open in shock

like a revelation

I saw that fire consuming me

and realized that
like suttee
like a zombie
I'd followed you into it
blindly

I recovered my will first

and with it
I stepped out of that
conflagration
and stared you down
until you went up
in smoke

and with determination
I began retrieving the rest of my
parts from the flames
smoldering hot
red and blue

I found my face and
was startled the first time
I was seen truly

I found my voice and felt
delight in its return
and amazement at
being heard

with each piece collected
I slowly reassembled
the constellation of
my being

each part had been tempered
by living breathing fire

and I saw that
I hadn't actually
burned
that instead I shone
like

Fierce
Stellar
Light

THE VOICE OF ERIN AURELIA

I call thunder to my side to
compliment my lightning

I call bowls of oceans to
catch my rain

I call the fecund earth to
receive
transmute
and regrow
my pain into
the beauty of petals
the allure of sepals
the sweetness of ripe fruit

I call the moon to reflect
the Light of my soul
back to me
and adore me
every night

I call the wind to me to
give me flight
to reveal wings from
underneath my skin

I call a cocoon to me so
my deepest
transformation

may finally begin

And I call fire to me—
that paramount transformer
that cosmic alchemist
that sorcerer of souls
that cunning high priestess

to bring me my death

to burn away my
flesh that hides the gleam of
my bones that house
quantum mysteries
untold

From within these flames
I call feathers to
adorn my form like
flickering light

and with these
wings I shall rise like
the hungry sun

to consume the
night

I THINK

I think in band names
        and bumper stickers,
in sad song titles and
        lamplight flickers

I think in poems
        and fetid praises,
in hallelujahs
        and lamentations

in river croons and
        hallucinations

in earth-deep sighs and
        contemplations

in cosmic cants and
        constellations

I think in heartbeats
        and the pulsar's quaver,
I think in the stone-speech
        which never wavers

I think in waves like
        tsunami swirls

I think in the twists a
        hurricane curls

I think in orbits
      mediating the sun,
I think in sunsets
      as the gloaming comes

I think in light animating
      life,
I think in famine, pestilence,
      and strife

I think in ribbons tying
      up time,
I think in devices dreaming
      up rhyme

I think in the voice of
      burgundy wine,
I think in symbols, fables,
      myths, and signs

I think in epic

I think in prose

I think in the hues of the
      clothes
dressing our
      souls
shining opaquely like
      gossamer gifts
         glowing bright

I think in the antique
        dishes furnishing our
                meals
I think in the medieval
        peals
of ancient bells
summoning the masses
                like a mystical
                        spell

I think in candles
        burnishing gold,
I think in haunted tales
        yet untold

I think in strains of distant
        laughter,
I think in the seductions of
        the ever-after

THE WILD

within me stirs flickers
        of flames longing for
            breath

a restless seed edgy
        and cagey, ready to
            jailbreak its tight
                cell

a rising tide, a swelling wave
        rushing to meet and touch
            the shore of the infinite

for I cannot be housed in
        a shell of mundanity

and the perpetual fire of
        my enduring soul cannot
            be quenched by forced

complicity with stipulations that
        would shackle my wild spirit

keep it chained to forces that
        would drain and bleed me to
            feed gaping maws that never
                know the satiation of

the flame that ascended heights
        to look upon the faces of stars

the wave that reached the wide and
       welcoming shore it sought and longed for

the seed that gorged itself on sunshine
       until it became what it was meant to be—

a magnificent being of
       form and light

PRINCESS

I'm so glad Princess Leia
is the Disney princess
I grew up with.

She didn't wait for boys to see her,

or demur when they spoke to her,

nor did she give them any more
daylight than she'd give anyone else.

She had things to do—
a Resistance to lead,
a planet and people to save,
dubiously short stormtroopers to question.

She didn't need any *man* for
courage or strength,

She *was* courage and strength.

So *why*
did the script tell her to
fall in love with
Han Solo—

the solo man, alone
in his emotional inaccessibility
and immaturity?

Why didn't the script tell her
that she knew better
than to fall for the rogue
whose flashing eyes and smile
held no promise
to reveal or share
anything meaningful?

He left her in the end,
after fully demonstrating his
ineptitude for human relationship,
and eating up her youth
in the process.

She *knew* all he loved was money.

She'd *said* so.

So she *did* know better than to
give herself to such a
dead heart
that knows someone loves him
but cannot reciprocate.

The men
who put that love
in her mouth

wanted to be fortunate enough
to be loved by a princess who

took no shit and
brooked no fools

but they didn't want to make themselves
worthy of her majesty.

So they taught us girls to
fall for men like them—
emotionally inept and void,

who desire beautiful countenances,
but need strong vessels into

which to pour all of
themselves
they don't want to carry

and instead demand that
we not break

while they

fill our holes.

VACANCY

Vacancy signs were hanging
      in my eyes

in all those photos
      from years past

my sum total appeared
      to be absence—

absent from myself
      and my fire

from the understanding
      that I would actually
            require my soul
                  to go any further

and not knowing it had
      been murdered,
            was being murdered
               every day,

that vacant was how he'd wanted me,
      so he could take up residence
            and hide any evidence of
               myself from me

Finally I learned to
      flee that scene of my
            death, and

resurrect breath back into my
      empty frame,

reclaim my name,
      accept that nothing was the same
            about where I'd been,
      trapped by him, and the
            pain blinding my sight,
      staining my eyes with
            the ink of all his lies
      that denied me the right
            to live in my skin with
                the way it sings,
      how it rings with the calling of
            falling stars I'd thought
                so far away

until finally I felt their
      heat warm my bones
            and reignite my soul

they took up space in his
      ousted place, and my spirit
            was revived,

no longer subsided into
      resignation,
no longer mired in murky
      stagnation,
no longer bound by assumed
      subjugation

and in my photos today
      I am delightfully taken by
            the reflected revivification
                of my visage,

Radiating the courage I
      found to inhabit myself
          like a gift
          like a presence
          like defiance

Like lions breaking free
      from cages,
and the certainty of knowing
      that I'll never wear vacancy signs
          in my eyes
              again

UNTILLED

I walk untilled
      unkilled
      unhindered
      by

the restriction of
      furrowed rows
      and the seeds of
            expectation

that assignment of
      ordained manifestation

and the pre-determination of

straight lines
like straight-jackets

shaving minds like a
straight-edge
of the
microbial dirt feathering
      all of our skins

I cannot begin
to
give in
to
the glamoury of

these untenable rules,
breaking my teeth
against rocks
against ploughs
against every cold steel
that would
unpeel the stars from
        my bones
and ravage my
        throat
while stealing my
        voice

that's bending like
    a river, falling from a
        defiant mountain

that will not hold
    false echoes

will not hold
    false hands holding
        false guns to my head

I cannot be killed

I will not be tilled

I will stare them all
    down with supernovas
        bleeding from my eyes

and unwind every
        breath suggesting
                that
        I should turn over
                my sod to feed
                        their gaping
                                mouths

LUGGAGE

It is not my job to wear
        your clothes, or fill
                the roles you've
                        assigned me

It is only my job to speak
        My Truth so firmly you'll
                have no choice but to
                        hear me

and if you deem my words
        the matches that burned
                everything down,

this fire's smoke will choke
        you as surely as 'round your
                neck is bound all the lies

you've told and must now
        bear, for I'll not be carrying

your luggage
with these hands

one
step
further

SHADOW

People see the smile that
      fills my face and reaches
          me eyes

and they think they know me.

They find me kind, assume I'm benign—

they underestimate me.

They don't realize that my
      rows of grinning teeth

comprise a line not to
      be crossed

and that behind their fence swells
      an ocean of salt-bitter tears

that the words I bite back are
      far more than the ample words
          I share

and that this visage of placid
      pleasantness they see is

a grate confining a conflagration
      of rage and desire whose sparks

might shoot out and land on
    them at any moment.

In this sense, a smile makes a
    great disguise, yet I don't
    mean it any less.

But for all the worlds erupting
    inside me, what should I show
    instead?

A smile is a ready one-size-fits-all
    face, universally palatable and
    easy to digest

doesn't challenge or defy or
    seek to define this space
        differently than you might

doesn't suggest that we may all
    be undone by the next incoming
    breath.

So a smile I'll wear because
    everything else is in the
        dirty laundry

and you're more than welcome
    to enjoy it.

But you'll understand it better

if you imagine the shadow

of a knife glittering
between my teeth

while you view it.

POOR

Mothering:
so noble
so brave
so All-American apple pie
yet a vocation unable
to receive even a
minimum wage.

Don't worry.
I'll stay poor for you.

You can serve as a soldier
for twenty years
make a career out of war
and destruction
and retire with a pension
and distinction
but mothers who served
just as long
fighting to raise healthy
caring adults to
serve us all
are consigned to
poverty.

Don't worry.
I'll stay poor for you.

Your lip service doesn't

pay my rent
doesn't even pretend
to value the time I've spent
in the daily minutia of
care and toil and
shit and snot and
feeding life.

Strife is valued far more
than what I have given.

Don't worry.
I'll stay poor for you.

SEDUCTION/ABDUCTION

Hades always lies
in wait, setting his
hellmouth trap
with blossomed

bait, floral-breathed
and petal-tongued, seducing

like heady poppies
drugging the air, flirting
like winking daisies weaving
into handcuffs, reaping

incandescent bodies with
sunflower-stalk scythes while
the innocently bystanding sky looks
on, indifferent, and the
clouds smirk

below the earth he hauled his
sweet prey, pressed his wet

seeds into trembling
hands until she
swallowed, stained her

legs with his sticky
juice, tattooed her flesh with

the sepulchral coneflower of
his sex, and her peeling skin began

to turn itself inside out, until

she wore her bones on
the outside like
battle armor
and

death became her native language

her beak-like phalanges pecked
and clawed at the walls of her
mineshaft of a prison, until

hidden seams yielded
their gleam, and, with the

heat of her Breath, worth
its weight in rubies, she forged

her emblem of Sovereignty,
crowning herself Queen of the Dead

slipping slim ivory carpals and
metacarpals between window bars,
she snapped off a dirk of an icicle,

deftly picked her lock, followed
vermillion-stained footprints to
his lair, to find him in bed

who knew deception
could sleep so

soundly like that, like
clean sheets unwrinkled, like
a virgin field unploughed, like
summer berries unplucked

with the precision of a
scalpel, she vivisects
his torso with her icicle, releasing wilted arsenals
of botanic ammunition, reeking
of opium and steel

there were no guts to be found

once serviceably disemboweled, to
ensure no demonic spirit
would stalk her steps, her icicle

claimed his eyes for her prize, becoming
her tokens of liberation to cross

the River Lethe
the river back to life and forgetfulness
of the realm of the dead

many moons later
she innocently walks and smiles in the
sunshine again, but finds she is

strangely nauseated by the
scent of pomegranates, and she

never trusts a man

bearing flowers

STRANGER

the present feels like
  a new acquaintance

the future like a
  stranger

Only inside music does
  my Now make sense
  feel familiar
  ground my being

If this song of my life
  can unwind itself one
    note at a time

then its rhythm can
  carry me

and its melody sing me
  into friendly seas
    under sunny skies

whose swells will lift me
  toward the stars
    and then perhaps

I'll realize

that I've known the tune

all along

COMBUSTION

part prayer, part spell

Eyes
like the sky

Heart like
a sunrise

I'll recognize you
        by your voice
        raining like falling
                stars
        covering me in light

I'll hear the sea when
        I hold you up to my
                ear

Washed-up treasure will
        appear in your wake

these earthquakes will
        still and the land
                will solidify

while your bones will
        ring in tune with mine
                and all of our pieces
                        will rhyme

Your embrace will taste
        of endlessness, of
                fountains that
        never run dry, of a fire that
                doesn't die

We'll move in time
        with the turning
                of the moon

There'll be no room
        for missteps, our
                rhythm will wax and
                        wane with our breath,
        and the rest of our orbits
                will glide like song-lines
                        circling the sun

Then we'll have begun
        to dance
in the utterance of infinity

Don't try to save me,
        don't be my hero

You be your planet, and
        I'll be mine

We're not here to be
        pulled like gravity
                into that black hole
                        of invisibility

You'll know my contours, and
     I'll know yours, and the same
          constellations shall illuminate
        our nights

We'll navigate by
    the stars
and ride cosmic
    winds
    like incantations
    where our
        declarations
    will become the
        birth of worlds
        coalescing
        into the form
        of our own making

ever-arising
    always becoming
        like a tune
            never-ending

It's not a destination
it's not a hard construction
it is the heat of

combustion

forever fueled by the
    connection between our
        Eyes

RETURN

the Stars, they lined up and sang to me
      in crystalline voices clear,
      like pealing bells of good tidings,
      in insistent tones of cosmic kennings,
         like wishes heard and held.

the Mountains, they opened up and sang to me
      with deep, resonant humming,
      thrumming with voices like earthquakes,
      vibrating through heart and mind,
         cleansing me of dross.

the Waters, they washed over me
      like tidal waves of time
      rinsing away everything that wasn't
         mine.

I rode each ripple as it gave itself away
      til tides picked me up
      and carried me—

Singing me
washing me
carrying me

Singing me
washing me
carrying me

Singing me
washing me
carrying me

back home

RECLAIMING

Retracing my steps
      I saw bloody footprints
            I hadn't known I'd left

my blood now a part
      of this place—it can't
            forget or erase me
                  it knows my scent

all my wishes started here
      like seeds in sidewalk cracks
            told one day they'd bloom
                bright like the sun

til someone called them weeds
      and ripped them from sustenance
            —little though it was

and I bled over the pavement like rain

now I reweave my way
      from my ground zero to
            my transplanted home

collecting these drops of blood
      like shining beads
          and

restringing them as i go
      making whole

the wounds

re-ordering the pattern
        into a constellation
               of life

to adorn my re-made self
        as I arrive in the world
            that
        awaits me now—

places that hold me
        eyes that see me
               arms that welcome me

and a garden about me
        in which to grow

LESS AND LESS

Opening my inbox one morning,
I was confronted with this:

"Do you over-apologize?"

I thought, *less and less.*

Do I over-apologize when someone hurts me?
Less and less.

Do I over-apologize when I've been misunderstood?
Less and less.

Do I over-apologize when I've been abandoned?
Less and less.

Do I over-apologize

when I dare speak the
words you shudder to hear

when I dare hold up a mirror
before your craven eyes

when I call to the skies to
rain justice for me
and down on you

when I plant my feet and

burst into bloom in
the place where life
intended me to be

when all the seeds in my soul
hitch a ride on subliminal winds
and tickle the skins of those I'm
meant to know

when my feet gather up courage
and speed
take destined steps
psychically

when the stars and the trees
tell me everything they know

and I believe them,

do I over-apologize?

Less and less and less
and less and less
and less and
less and
less

THE BLACK EVERYTHING

like stars, we float through
the black everything

shining like pinpoints of
        light shot through a
                cosmic blanket

the magic carpet upon
        which we all ride into
                mysteries and marrow

and the entropy we swallow
        when we cannot fathom the
                endlessness that gathers

us up like eggs in a basket
        or bones in a grave

the black everything enfolds
        us and arranges our space

while it chortles at our
        distorted perception of time

knowing inwardly that only
        rhyme holds the universe
                in place

and only one ridiculously

misplaced beat would
       render all that connects

us to come undone like
      a snagged thread tearing
         a hole in your favorite

winter sweater that holds warm
      darkness against your skin

the breath of life would be
      lost to that gaping wound

along with sound and lungs and
      larynxes and bodies so that

nothing would be left to

sing it whole

REVOLVING DOOR

Every darkness feels like a tomb
an ending bleak and desolate
but in its quiet death
it becomes a womb.

We mourn what leaves too soon
weep the tears of the disconsolate
soul grieving beside the
all-consuming tomb.

Though this moment of doom
seems to our spirit inviolate
loss brings life
so creates a womb.

For the void fills us with a new bloom
like springtime
fertile and temperate
and what is this but a womb?

While darkness can tear us in two
remember that this is definite:

That the place of ending
that shapes a tomb
houses the seeds of rebirth
so is also a womb.

LOVE THE WOUND

Love the wound
    beneath the skin
        buried in caverns
            of calcium
        deep in dark folds of
            bone

Love the wound that
    gapes as a fathomless
        chasm
    retract the damage that
        rendered it so by
        leaving its debris
            in a field with a
            headstone

Love the wound
    that weeps like
        sweet water welling
            from rock
        as it trickles down dank
            cave walls
            wailing and forlorn

Love the wound
    as it keens like
        wild wind, unwinding
            every blow endured
            by wrathful words from
            soulless men

Love the wound
      love the taste of sorrow
           it bears like the remembered
                flavor of union pledged by
                    resonance alone

Love the wound
how it breaks skin and bone
breaks the heart
breaks our masks
'til they fall apart

breaks tenacious flesh
clinging to its frame beneath
housing seams of gold
treasure untold

the truth of a light we
      can only behold when
           the dressing disguising
           it is peeled away, thus removing
                our blinders that keep us from
                    seeing true

Love the wound
      for the gift it brings
      for the incandescence its
           cracks will reveal

Love the wound
      and the pain of its
           tearing

Love the wound
        and the blood as its
                flowing

Love the wound
        for the disease it is
                purging

Love the wound
        and the end it is
                making

Love the wound
        for the poison it is
                taking out of your
                        soul

So that all the old
        forms may be utterly
                shaken

Because only once they
        have finally fallen will
                we know how we are
                        truly whole

SOVEREIGN

—a song

Verse 1

You used me up
You bled me dry
You called it love
You fed me lies

You burned me down
You razed my soul
Then I rose again
finally whole

Chorus

All those days I lived in the black
All those days I'll never get back
From your destruction I had to flee
Like the risen sun
I am finally free

Never again
Never again
Never again

Verse 2

My path is my own now,
free of your malice
I'm in control and will
build my own palace

Only those I allow
shall pass through its door
and Sovereign I'll be here
forevermore

Chorus
All those days I lived in the black
All those days I'll never get back
From your destruction I had to flee
Like the risen sun
I am finally free

Never again
Never again
Never again

I AM THE RIVER

after Chris Cornell, with loud love

I am not these broken pieces,
        I am the solid core

 I am not this washed-up
        detritus on the shore,
                I am the swelling sea

I am not these refractions
        of shattered light,
                I am the defiant star

I am not these tracts of
        scars running over my skin,
                I am the new growth glowing
                        over them

I am not the moon coldly
        orbiting and reflecting,
                I am the Sun

I am not these passing clouds
        gathering cumulonimbusly,
                I am the sky

I am not that razed building
        smoldering in ruins,
                I am the cleared ground

I am not those hot ashes,
     I am the fire

I am not this despair
     that overtakes me,
          I am the desire

I am not the carnage
     rotting in the heat,
          I am the lion

I am not the spent foliage
     littering the forest floor,
          I am the tree

I am not the shipwrecked
     sailor held captive by the waves,
          I am the island he sees

I am not the raw verbiage
     scattered across this paper,

I am the page

turning
     turning
          turning

into a new chapter
     yet unwritten

I am not the actor uttering
      premeditated lines,
            I am the stage

I am not these tears
      that threaten to drown,

I am the mighty river

that feeds all
      carries all

changes all

in each shifting moment
      through time

EPILOGUE

"I took a deep breath and listened to the old brag of my heart.
I am, I am, I am."
—Sylvia Plath, *The Bell Jar*

ABOUT THE AUTHOR

 Erin Aurelia is a poet, author, editor, and book coach.

She is the author of *The Torch of Brighid: Flametending for Transformation*, and has been published in anthologies by Moon Books and Goddess Ink.

As Erin R Lund she is co-author of the Amazon international best-seller, *Get Published: Industry Experts Share Their Secrets*, and is named by LA Weekly as one of their "15 Book Coaches to Watch in 2023." She is owner and CEO of Sunshine Editorial Services & Book Coaching, where she specializes in editing nonfiction books in the genres of memoir, self-help, personal development, alternative spirituality, and holistic wellness. As a book coach, she helps soul-centered coaches, healers, and therapists write client-attracting, transformational books to amplify their authority, build their businesses, and impact lives.

Bone & Stars: A Constellation of Poems of Recovery and Healing from Narcissistic Abuse is her first published volume of poetry.

Erin is mother to two grown sons and lives in Vancouver, Washington, with more books than she'll complete reading in this lifetime. And yes, she will buy more. Find her around town performing at open mics and in shows accompanied by her favorite local musicians.

Find Erin Aurelia online at

https://www.sunshineeditorialservices.com/erin-aurelia-poet

Follow her on social media to read her latest work and watch videos of her spoken-word performances at

https://www.facebook.com/erinaureliapoetry

and

https://www.instagram.com/erinaureliapoetry

If you or anyone you know is experiencing domestic abuse of any kind, find support at your local YWCA.

https://www.ywca.org/what-we-do/health-safety/domestic-and-sexual-violence-services

www.ingramcontent.com/pod-product-compliance
Lightning Source LLC
Chambersburg PA
CBHW070920120626

46546CB00001B/341